Daddy's Little Girl

To Jerry, With Love

Lilian Grace

Daddy's Little Girl

Lilian Grace

authorHOUSE®

AuthorHouse™
1663 Liberty Drive
Bloomington, IN 47403
www.authorhouse.com
Phone: 1-800-839-8640

© 2015 Lilian Grace. All rights reserved.

No part of this book may be reproduced, stored in a retrieval system, or transmitted by any means without the written permission of the author.

Published by AuthorHouse 1/8/2015

ISBN: 978-1-4969-6276-8 (sc)
ISBN: 978-1-4969-6277-5 (e)

Library of Congress Control Number: 2015900150

Any people depicted in stock imagery provided by Thinkstock are models, and such images are being used for illustrative purposes only. Certain stock imagery © Thinkstock.

This book is printed on acid-free paper.

Because of the dynamic nature of the Internet, any web addresses or links contained in this book may have changed since publication and may no longer be valid. The views expressed in this work are solely those of the author and do not necessarily reflect the views of the publisher, and the publisher hereby disclaims any responsibility for them.

Contents

Foreword: First, a Prayer xi
Acknowledgments xiii
Chapter 1: Crossroads 1
Chapter 2: Mommy Issues 5
Chapter 3: The Monster 9
Chapter 4: Addiction 22
Chapter 5: Rebound Man 28
Chapter 6: Hard Times 40
Chapter 7: Skeletons in the Closet 48
Chapter 8: It's all about the Recovery 51

Having no face to view
The window inside her soul
Lying wounded and defeated
Her heart stained and blackened
Like a piece of burnt coal

Discolored by circumstance
Nature's beauty summons Thee
Freedom awaits His good grace
Wishing this rescue sets her free

Princess of privilege
Casting all betrayal away
Trusting the voices in her dreams
She crossed a bridge and left home that day

Floating away to find her destiny
Riding a rainbow to a wish
Swinging on the ropes of faith
To encounter love again, that first kiss

Let the rains fall down
Cleanse this fragile being
Lead her to an eternal balance
Have mercy, her wings are bleeding

LILIAN GRACE

A shadow of a butterfly
Whispers in the breeze
Fragrance of fresh blossoms
Awakening to rise up off her knees

Harmony in the dawn of a new day
Waterfalls carry her up stream
Escaping all eternal fears
She built a new home
From all those hopes and dreams

Chris Grey   1934–1977

Floating Away
Up and over a rainbow
Addictions left behind
Cutting loose ropes of sorrow

Drifting farther away
Ignorant that you had died
Your body laid down to rest
Not given a chance to say good-bye

Walk gently on each stepping stone
Looking for the truth in Him
I'll pray in His name
Have mercy, forgiving all eternal sins

Farewell, my dear friend
The curtain closed too soon
When our journey ends
And our paths cross

We'll dance under the same moon

Shain Carruthers   1971–2010

Foreword

FIRST, a PRAYER

Dear Lord,

I am scared, but I trust you. I am weak, so very drained, and I need you to wrap your wings of love around me. I know there is a greater purpose, but I am only as you have made me. Please hear my prayers, Lord, and heal the sickness that plagues me. Allow me to feel within this tired and bruised body of pain. I pray that you will have mercy upon me and grant me the strength to be a stronger soldier in your vast army of true believers. I am scared, Lord, but my trusted faith grows stronger knowing your blessings of warmth will protect me from myself. I ask you, Lord, to have mercy upon this child of misfortune. I relinquish my burdens of grief upon your shoulders. Bless me with the love of your guidance, clothe me with the courage of armor for this battle, and provide my soul the food for reason. Please keep me humble, Lord, and allow me to receive the true gifts you have blessed me with from the beginning of my existence. May my presence here on earth shine through to the heavens above, and may I be worthy of your praise.

Amen.

Acknowledgments

Brandon,

Thank you for being there from the beginning. Without your support and input, this would not have been possible.

Michael,

Thank you for all of your unconditional love and support in my life, including your support to create this novel.

Ruby V,

Thank you for always supporting me throughout my life's journey.

Ian and Carmen

Thank you for always being there to bend an ear or provide a shoulder to lean on.

Chapter 1
CROSSROADS

Daddy's little girl:
Her hair full of bows and curls;
Watch them dance and twirl.

My name is Lilian and over twenty-five years ago, I was a nineteen-year-old woman enrolled in college. I worked weekends for extra cash, and I was involved in a common-law relationship. I found myself content even though my future felt unclear. I had no real direction in terms of what would come next, and I had no plan to execute any long-term goals. I should have had more pride at that time in my life.

My entire world changed one spring day in March of 1991. It was the day my father passed away. He had been fighting cancer for the past three years, and the battle ended when he was a sixty-three-year-old man. It was time for change, a time to find out where people in the family ranked on the totem pole of responsibility and respect. I became a slave as I mourned the loss of my dad, and I became numb to all the complicated emotions. I felt like a strip had been taken off of me that left a huge hole in my existence. Foreign feelings of loss, abandonment, and everything in between rushed upon me, and they demanded answers to questions that I couldn't wrap my brain around. I was extremely vulnerable; I longed for the entire mess to be nothing more than a horrific nightmare. My mother, older brother, aunt, and everyone in the immediate family who had a notch to claim on that totem pole mourned the loss of my father with tremendous grief. But of all the cast and crew involved, Dad and I shared a special connection unlike any of the other family members. I was proud of my title: *Daddy's little girl.*

There are priceless memories that have stayed nestled in my heart. As Daddy's little girl, I could always be found hanging out with him: spending time in his workshop playing darts, listening to Jim Reeves and Charlie Pride on the old 8-track tapes, waxing toboggans for the midnight snow runs, or sipping the suds that came off of the beer bottle he just opened. I really missed spending time with him when I was at school, figure skating, attending ballet classes, practicing the piano, or on a track-and-field trip. One could say that my mom kept me very busy.

My dad always made me laugh, and I always felt secure. Christmas was always a time I looked forward to. Going back into the bush and cutting down a tree for the house was always special. The smell filled our home with a scent that brought me back to the time when I still believed in Santa. The memories of his barbecues, freshly baked apple pies, and joke-telling reminds me what a wonderful, caring father I had. His gardens were incredible, his carpentry work was flawless, and his ability to allow my mother to disrespect him without causing damage to his kids was undeniably selfless. My favorite pastime was playing catch with him. I still have the glove he gave me when I was only nine. Once in a while, it gets dusted off and used; otherwise, I just think back to those fond memories that are a part of who I am.

One Saturday morning, I awoke to my mother ripping out the curlers she had so brutally put in my hair the night before. She was always trying to make me look like a girl. My dad was off to the bush to cut down a few trees and haul the wood back to the house. It was a cheaper way to heat the house at the time. We never complained about being cold as long as my dad was in charge of stoking the old, cast-iron stove. I ran out the door as mother was putting a pretty, green bow in my hair. I flagged my dad down and joined him in the bush that day, curls and all. He loved it. I was the son he never had—despite the fact that my brother was five years older than me. I was a tomboy and proud of it! He was a generous soul, and he loved to cook for the family. He was the fixer in the family, and I truly believed that there wasn't anything he couldn't do. He was my hero then, and he is my hero now. He shared a solid relationship with me, one that any girl who was growing up could count on.

We are all faced with a great event or a fork in the road; we are all forced to make a choice at one point or another. Indeed, these choices can affect the entire outcome of one's personal journey. It has been more than twenty-five years since I found myself at a crossroads. I was stubborn and arrogant. The right and left turns that I chose to take were not very nurturing or smart. Still, my journey down that road turned me into who I am today. Those wrong turns haunt me today. I often hear those fateful words echoing through space: "If only I knew back then what I know now, my life would be much different and better today." I would be healthier, wealthier, and happier. Instead of being a high school dropout, I would have graduated and traveled the world, soaking up all it had to offer. I would have had a relationship that wasn't forced or manipulated. I would have had a relationship that would continue to grow and support a more stable version of myself and my partner. Instead, I settled for a possessive, disrespectful psychopath.

I was only a sixteen-year-old girl when we hooked up, and my dad was not impressed with the choice I had made. I now understand why. It broke his heart to see that I was willing to settle for a control freak who would eventually take away everything he wanted for his little girl.

Chapter 2

MOMMY ISSUES

Cruel Expectations

Why don't you see?
I'm only a child, look at me!
Expectations stare through your eyes;
You're disappointed; however, I've paid the price.

Failure is not an option,
Not permitted to cry—
You robbed me of those tender moments;
Your cruelty made sure I was denied.

Loyal and true,
I sacrificed my happiness for you.
Locked away an ocean of tears;
Irony is owned by your own fears.

Your attention misplaced elsewhere,
Today we have a second chance.
You turn your back,
You walk away without a good-bye glance

Despite your morality—
Gross nurturing, too—
I was taught to love one another.
Miraculously enough, I still do

After my dad's funeral service, I continued to mourn the loss. My mother had her own idea about closure and what she needed to accomplish. She seemed to be struggling with her own fears when she reached that fork in the road. Would she choose to continue a routine that didn't exist anymore now that dad was gone? Or would she choose to become a free woman, who wouldn't make the sacrifices necessary for marriage? I could tell that the grief from the loss was eating her up inside. Her own future, though, was all she appeared to care about. She took little comfort in the reality that I was suffering, too.

My grief didn't need to be dismissed (and certainly not minimized). After all, I was only a seventeen-year-old girl when she decided to leave our family for a three-year contract that entailed working and residing in the Middle East. It was an opportunity for her to make more money and further her career. She couldn't do that in Canada, where it was much more difficult to reach the top in her field. She had worked hard her entire life, and she was still not content. It was an old desire of hers to work overseas.

My parents had the kind of relationship in which my dad respected Mom's career and never held her back from all she dreamed of doing. Her career was always her first priority in life. She would promise to go away for a short stint. Dad held down the fort and waited faithfully for her return. Ironically enough, within the first two months of Mom gone and working, Dad was diagnosed with multiple myeloma. With the cancer in its third stage, the doctor anticipated my dad would have only three years left to live.

Unfortunately, my mom signed a formal contract, and she was not permitted to leave under any circumstances. Recruitment offices out of the United States signed individuals up for two- or three-year terms. The authorities held her passport, and that was the way it was. I was the one who phoned her overseas to deliver the terrible news.

After my dad's passing, my mother decided to make an announcement that there was nothing left to keep her in Canada. I remember thinking, *What a selfish bitch! Thanks a lot for caring. Don't you care about me? Why are you disregarding the unity of our family? After all, I think everyone concerned was overwhelmed with the death of Dad.* The tissues were still being handed out when she decided to leave and start a new life for herself. During a three-week period, I lost my dad *and* my mom.

It was time to assume the role of responsibility because Mom left us behind. I would step into my father's shoes to fill the position that was available on our family's totem pole. Because my dad and mom owned a rather large house on an acre of high-maintenance property, I was rather thrilled that Mom asked me to take care of the family's best interest. I could manage a home, yard work, animals, financial decisions, and my dad's sister, who lived in the basement suite. I could handle being a gardener, a college student, and a girlfriend.

I didn't realize at the time that I could have chosen a different path; I could have spread my wings to fly. All I was doing was entertaining other people's dreams and giving them the freedom to do so. After all, nobody told me about my new responsibilities. I didn't put it all together until a few years ago. I was suffering with my mommy issues, and it took me a long time to arrive at the truth.

I know I was a late bloomer, but give me a break! I was given our family estate, vehicles, and an old lady in the basement. She was my dad's older sister, and she was a diabetic and legally blind. She was very needy. I had my whole life ahead of me, but I had always valued my family and wanted to do the right thing. When I look back now, I shake my head. What was I thinking?

Chapter 3

THE MONSTER

By April, my boyfriend and I had moved into my parents' home. It was a quick decision, and we packed up the apartment where we were currently living in short order. My mom was reassured that the family estate would be in good hands. Therefore, she decided to go back overseas to reach her professional goals. She wanted a better-paying job and a higher position in the medical field. Although I was torn with emotional loss and abandonment, moving back home made the mourning a little easier. I felt respected with a higher rank on the family's totem pole. All I had to do was look around to see the memories Dad had left behind, and I was content. Although my common-law relationship was abusive, I thought the new chapter would give our relationship the security and respect I needed.

I was so, so wrong, and there would be no happy ending for me. It would just turn out to be a delusional fantasy. The more I gave, the more he took—nothing was good enough for him. He was a monster from the beginning. He controlled our situation and acted as if he were responsible and deserved all the credit for all I had just inherited. Actually, it was my mother's generosity that gave us the great opportunity. It was a chance to build a life together without the hurdles and obstacles most young couples encounter. We had a home, property, new vehicles, and no debt. I had a huge responsibility to make sure everything was maintained sufficiently. I felt I had something to prove, and I wanted to show my mom that I could handle it. The whole thing seemed like an excellent idea at the time.

If I had a chance to do it all over again knowing what I know now, would I? Would I again choose to support an individual who continually abused me in one form or another? Would I take the other turn on the pathway through my life's journey? Would I continue to put myself second and remain loyal to a man who wound up being undeserving of my love? Would I turn a blind eye to harm and corruption? That I ignored rational thinking is hard to understand.

I knew that the moral steps to take entailed getting engaged and married. I thought that was what my boyfriend and I had been working toward for the past four years. He had the courtesy to ask my dad for my hand in marriage on his death bed. My dad gave him his blessing even though he wanted a better life for me. After all, Dad knew what I wanted. He was dying and there wasn't much he could do. There was no ring, no proposal—just more abusive behavior that devastated me time and time again. It was my mom who gave me my grandmother's wedding rings. He didn't even bother to thank her. He was happy enough not having to spend the money on me. I wonder whether he married me out of pity, or whether he was just selfish.

When I was twenty, I dedicated my life to a man who hurt me emotionally, morally, mentally, physically, and sexually. I had a misguided belief that if I promoted a commitment to positive actions, love, and support, I would receive that same trust and respect.

I grew up as a Christian, and I still believe in treating others as you would like to be treated. I thought he would love me as I loved him. I convinced myself in my heart and in my mind that he would eventually see the light and settle into a monogamous relationship with me. My reward for being loyal and faithful was a mixed bag of STDs, broken teeth, broken bones, black eyes, lies, and humiliation. I was the woman in the emergency ward of the hospital covering up her partner's abusive behavior.

He was always so angry and in the mood to argue—even if there was nothing to argue about. I remember him coming at me without warning and punching me square in the face as if I were a man. Defending myself would only make matters worse, I knew, and I ended up on the floor with his hands around my neck choking me until I almost lost consciousness. If I fought back, he would break my fingers and beat me worse. If I tried to run away, he would rip the clothes off my back and steal my purse. I was the woman who answered the door and created stories when the police came on a disturbance call. Honestly, I was stupid! I actually thought no other man would love me or want to be with me. I put him on a pedestal and worshipped the ground he walked on. Casts, crutches, tears, and makeup continued to cover up my brutal reality.

I was ordered to clean the house and make sure it was next to perfect for him and his friends. I wasn't permitted to have my own friends or go anywhere to do anything without his approval or accompanying me. He expected me to work more and have a higher income so he didn't have to work. If I had any friendships, it was understood that he could and would have sex with them in front of me. Though I must have had rocks in my head, I truly felt sorry for him. I loved him more than I loved myself. I always thought that, one day, it would be better. He always apologized and promised me it would never happen again. I believed him. My love was unconditional.

Denial became a major issue in my life. What a waste of time and energy. I gave what should have been some of the best years of my life to a monster.

I became controlled as his possessive behavior became worse and more violent. My screaming could be heard from the surrounding homes. There was always one neighbor that would call the authorities. Knocks on the door from the police broke up the madness he poisoned our lives with. He knew that the cops couldn't enter without a warrant. Back then, the police didn't even have the authority to arrest an individual who was harming his spouse. On one occasion that the police showed up, I was tied up and muffled in the closet. The door was slammed in their face, and there wasn't a damn thing they could do about it. Can you believe this excuse for a man laughed and talked about it for the remainder of the evening as he untied me before kissing me good night? I can't believe that choking me half to death was not enough for me to leave. Rather, I felt that, somewhere inside him, there was a good person. I was deep in the cycle of abuse, and that lasted for an additional twelve years.

In 1993, my husband, The Monster, was injured at work, on the job site. He claimed that a coworker injured his lower back. I was pregnant then, which was bad timing because when he wasn't working, he was contributing even less to our relationship (let alone the household). The income I was supporting us with was not high enough. We were living paycheck to paycheck, but with a baby on the way, I was trying to put money in the cookie jar, too. He milked the situation for all it was worth. He claimed he was unable to walk because his back hurt him so much; however, he was always out and about and enjoying himself. I remained home, cleaning and making sure the yard work was done. The physical abuse ceased when I was pregnant, but the verbal abuse was just as severe. He allocated funds that I had saved for the birth of our baby and bought a brand new dirt bike with all the safety equipment and gear. He claimed that he had little joy in his life because he was injured, and he said the least I could do was support his decision and accept the large purchase he had made.

I had no choice but to sit down, shut up, and take it. I was about to give birth and didn't want to risk him causing harm to me or my unborn baby. I became stressed out, and I wondered how I was going to manage all the responsibilities necessary to raise a child. My mother's generosity funded absolutely everything we needed for my son's nursery. She was so good to us, and he was so ungrateful. He acted as if he deserved the handout because he was giving her a grandchild despite not wanting children himself. In his twisted mind, he figured my mom was the one who should be grateful.

Four months after my son was born, I really started to panic. The three of us were home together, and my maternity benefits were running out. I was most concerned about my son and how I could provide a stable lifestyle for him. I knew his father wasn't going to help; he didn't care as long as he got what he wanted. It was then that I asked The Monster whether I could return to work. I wanted to start my own business to make up for his laziness and inability to support his family. He told me that I was allowed to work if I took care of our son, too. After all, he didn't change diapers. Who was he kidding? He didn't do much of anything!

Nevertheless, I agreed because I thought I could make it work despite his conditions. I was eager to get out of the house and make something of myself that my son could be proud of. I opened up the cupboard below my kitchen sink, grabbed all the cleaning supplies I owned at the time, and hit the pavement. I began going door to door and asking businesses whether they were looking for a cleaning lady. Within a couple of days, I started to work. Within one year, I had enough work to start hiring other people. After two years, I had a solid foundation built, an office in my home, and a husband who still refused to work. I had worked around each customer's strict schedule and built my business up from there. I did very well, even with The Monster continuously on my back.

As the business grew, so did I. It was the best thing I could have done for my son and myself! I began to evolve and reinvent myself. By the year 2000, I was a thirty-year-old woman, and I was beginning to open my eyes and change. I was growing and developing into a successful business woman; however, my personal life was still quite challenging.

There are memories that will haunt me for a very long time. Some memories are still vivid despite finalizing our divorce long ago. The shadows that darken the innocence in people is brutal. I remember suitcases being thrown at me during my first honeymoon night, threats of divorce from the beginning, and being passed around to his friends during drunken gatherings. I also recall cocaine abuse and infidelity. Those are just a few things that I endured. There was no respect, and I started to realize there never would be. When I was Daddy's little girl I never expected my husband to ask me to expose myself and flash my breasts for his friends. Humiliation, yes; disgust with my husband, absolutely.

I didn't understand why the person I chose to spend my life with had no regard for the sacred term: *wife*. I was an object used for his sick amusement. Sadly enough, I cooperated. I was stuck in a world of pleasing others, trying to be the good wife, but all I did was risk my own principles, morals, and sanity.

It took me a total of fifteen years—starting in 1986—to leave him. Eventually, with God's strength, I walked away and never looked back. Before that, I found myself begging God to help me escape the arms of the man I knew didn't love me. I asked God to give me the strength required to make an honest decision that I could feel comfortable with and walk away without too much heartache. I was stronger than I ever gave myself credit for.

But until then, I had forgotten about loving myself and being true to myself. I enabled him to control and punish me. His own guilt was buried deep within our relationship. I think he was trying to make up for being inadequate in terms of size and life. For him to admit the truth, he would have to admit to being a monster. Projecting his anger upon me and turning the table of lies around was much safer for him. He could never own up to his mistakes. After all, he had it made in the shade with me. The more I gave, the more he took. Eventually, nothing was good enough for my pathetic husband.

These were the stepping stones of our relationship. I honestly believed that, one day, he would be grateful for me. One thing I knew was that I didn't envision such a life for myself when I was Daddy's little girl.

Did anything good come from this horror show? You bet! I have been blessed with a beautiful, kind, and loving son. He is the reason for my happiness. So if I had to do it all over again, I would (for the most part). I learned to make a promise to myself: I would never allow another person to treat me so poorly. I vowed to raise my son with the love from my heart, not the terror from his father. It was easier to be a single mom than to put my seven-year-old child in the pathway of abuse. After all, murder is illegal. My son was so innocent and full of love. He wanted our approval desperately, and he didn't understand the hostility coming from his father.

I remember one time I found myself exhausted by work and exhausted as a parent. I asked The Monster to relieve me for an hour, and he said, "You know I never wanted children. Deal with it!" As hard as that was to hear, I did just that. I only wished our son had had two parents who loved and nurtured him instead of just one. After all, he didn't ask to be brought into this world. The older my son became, the tougher The Monster was on him. He would not excuse the small things that all children do. Often, my son touched things in the house because he was learning to walk. At that point, The Monster flung his knuckles at his child's head to correct him. This broke my heart, and I knew I had to find an exit.

I didn't want my child to suffer the wrath of his father. He would have thought it was his fault, and that is far from the truth! I had grown a lot through my business and began to realize that I didn't need a jerk dictating my every move. The more I grew, the more he became threatened. Eventually, I was able to make a decision for my son that I knew would be healthier in the long run. Leaving The Monster was the best decision I ever made. The feeling of liberation was overwhelming! I couldn't wait until I was out on my own to make my own choices (and mistakes). I was a thirty-one-year-old woman who was finally living without any misguided or hostile intentions.

With a lot of persistence, dedication, prayer, and wrong turns, I started to overcome the brainwashing that The Monster had instilled in me. With a few years of therapy for me and my son, I reached closure on that chapter in our lives. My son understood that his father had lied to him about our divorce. He came to the conclusion that I wasn't the "evil bitch" that destroyed our family. I thank the Lord for not only hearing my prayers, but also for answering them. Finally, the cycle of abuse had been broken.

I heard people mentioning that girls always married people like their fathers. I wished that was true for me; I married my mother. There are two differences between them: The Monster didn't fly in on his broomstick, and my mother had a heart of gold.

Broken Love

No mistaking the soul of a heart.
Games and lies leave blood stains
On a symbol made for love.

The sorrow that binds within
Marks a grave on the soul;
Ignorance and blindness become
The lonely for a tombstone with no name.

The grip of trust binding
Tears and sorrow remains trapped,
Desperate for an internal release.
Love becomes the broom,
Sweeping away the dust of ignorance.

Married to skepticism,
Widowed by the darkness of days past,
Forbidden is the clarity of happiness.
Saddened with obsessions,
Self-punishment fulfills
The regression of a life.

Daddy's Little Girl

Dusk lying still, unable to breathe,
The day weeping with regret,
Dismissing the tragedy of night
Only to repeat the twilight hour.

Haunted by one's own mistress,
Belonging to a broken soul:
Hidden strength is found.

Trust and gratitude will discover
An unfamiliar certainty.
A new kind of truth.

Chapter 4

ADDICTION

Ropes of Pain

Knots consumed by this monster
Contribute to the diseased soul;
No escape from this black plague,
No defense from the seeds it sows.

Intolerable, suffering bastard.
Silent is the thief in the night.
Inner pillar of strength shredded;
Blinded with no perspective in sight.

The hangers weigh heavy
In the closet of pain:
Nothing left to lose;
Nothing left to gain.

Unable to continue a journey,
Haunted by the purity of truth—
These masks worn on tormented souls.
Who has nothing left to prove?

Becoming one with the darkness,
The addict prowls the night.
Afraid to open tired eyes,
Unable to face what is hidden in the light.

Foundation's core rots inside;
Ignorance's is the prowler's game.
Unable to hear the tremor's shake,
Burnt bridges become the shame.

It's a reoccurring dream that haunts one's inner fears, leaving one hostage to the mortality and twisted desires of one's own mind. I wonder whether we should believe that dreams are a recreation of many voices that exist within our subconscious minds. Do we justify our personal failures? Do we only allow true happiness to reside in our dreams? Does our subconscious know something our conscious mind does not? Along with hope, why do our biggest fears also arise in a place meant for rest and rejuvenation? I think it's strange that this period of time used for relaxation can produce the kind of fear that makes one jump outside one's own skin. I think, maybe, we are our own worst enemies and prisoners within ourselves—gates, fences, and walls to block out any bad traffic that might come our way. It seems to be the defense system we use. But how do we really protect ourselves?

Anyone who has ever suffered with addiction knows what it feels like at 4:30 a.m. on any given day. Addiction is a nasty way of living, and it entered my life at age fifteen. At that time, I started smoking pot. By the time I was twenty, I had a daily marijuana habit, and I used cocaine on a regular basis. Alcohol, drugs, sex, gambling, and bad behavior are just a few examples of simple pleasures getting out of hand. I have found that some addictions synergize with each other. It's the ugly reality of an abusive, spinning wheel. There's no escaping to dreamland; there's no avoiding harsh consequences. I have found that nothing good can come from this type of behavior.

There came a time when my needs were selfish and self-serving—I didn't care what anyone had to say. If I wanted their opinion, I would gladly give it to them. That's a part of the ugliness that surfaces when the cycle of abuse spins the wheel. One consequence is that the chains of bondage start to hold the wrong prisoner captive … and the addiction holds the key. We all suffer one way or another. It's not just the addict in that dark and dismal place. It's like a black plague that infests one's entire life. People struggle with acceptance and dishonesty along with ignorance and disbelief. Betrayal and heartache fall heavy on their shoulders, too.

As for me, I think that all the baggage I claimed with my mommy and monster issues led me down a different pathway during my life's journey. It seemed like a good idea at the time. I was just trying to have fun by doing the few things I hadn't experienced yet—things I had missed out on when I became involved with The Monster as a sixteen-year-old girl. After leaving my husband, it was time for my wings to spread. I wanted to experience what the world had in store for me. I had never been so excited to reinvent my life. I was a free agent, and I was free from my abuser. Besides the day my son was born, I had never been happier.

In 2001, I remember skipping down a busy street in the city. I was on my way to get my first tattoo. I felt like I was making my first decision on my own in a long time. I didn't have anyone influencing or guiding me. I was new and improved, and I began letting my hair down for a change. I was going out and enjoying some of the fun the world had to offer. I liked the night scene, and I frequented many clubs. I partied a lot! I picked up strippers and consumed enough alcohol and weed to get a small tribe wasted. I lost sight of what I wanted to correct for my son and myself. Because one thing leads to another, vices seem to pop up more and more.

In the past, The Monster and I smoked on a daily basis. We binged on alcohol, and we enjoyed mixing it with what we called our social life. Excluding my immediate family, everyone we knew was a stoner. The weekend ritual entailed sitting in a circle and smoking joint after joint until the room was hot boxed (so full of smoke one can't see the others in the circle). I experimented with heavy drugs, such as cocaine, too.

Life started to spin out of control when our future paychecks were already promised to drug dealers. We made promises that were more than difficult to keep. Nobody's legs were broken, but I often wonder what we were thinking.

After becoming a free agent in the universe, there was another choice that presented its ugly face to me. I had last used that sort of drug eleven years prior. I had been clean since I was a twenty-year-old woman, but I was offered cocaine once again at a club in the restroom. Actually, I was in a stall with another girl. It was the beginning of the end of everything I had worked for and accomplished.

Looking back, I can see how I was and why that attracted certain people into my life. Justifying myself and convincing anyone who questioned my lifestyle became a habit in its own right. I was just having some fun. But like a thief in the night—and before I knew it—I was robbed and stripped of my dignity. I did see it coming; however, I ignored the warning signs as my addiction became worse. People started looking at me differently.

The Monster then took my son away from me, and all I wanted to do was retaliate! *It's The Monster who should be in the spotlight,* I thought. He was guilty of using drugs, too, after all. Plus, he was abusive. I remember thinking, *how dare they talk about me like that!* I was a good mother, but I was a good mother who had made mistakes. The worst part about my situation was that the monster was using my lowest point to execute his revenge plan on me.

He didn't care about my son's welfare—not when we were together, and surely not when we were apart. His agenda was to try to hurt me the way I hurt him. It was my son who wound up suffering and paying the price for the choices his parents made. I'll never forget the way my heart dropped on the floor after my son stated that he wanted to live with his dad. Despite being absolutely devastated, I also agreed with him. I knew The Monster would never change. I thought it might be a good time for my son to find out the facts about his dad. I wasn't in any position to argue, anyway.

Losing my son led me to pick myself up and dust myself off. At that point, I was seeing things more clearly. However, I needed to clean up the mess I had created. I had one priority: to get my son back.

Chapter 5

REBOUND MAN

I Speak My Truth

I was looking for love,
For a brave soul.
I went looking for you;
I didn't want to lose control.

Walking down the aisle,
I knew it wouldn't last:
Too much baggage
I carried from my past.

Your own shortcomings
Came out in a rush.
The relationship suffered,
Ending in dust.

Our relationship toxic,
Your mind so insane;
Tears of an endless waterfall—
You chose cocaine.

Forget about any friendship—
Separate lives we lead.
All that I'm interested in
Is watching you bleed.

Again, I gave
All that one could give.
In turn, the wheels spun ugly;
You didn't even want to live.

Jumping through hoops,
Rings of fire,
I couldn't even trust you.
You became such a liar.

Was it my fault?
Or are you to blame?
Today, I'm wondering
What we have gained.

Relationships always start out with that hot, sexy passion that lasts all night. You become a slave to your desires *and* your partner's desires. If only that ecstasy could last, most of us who chose to be in a monogamous relationship would be happy.

My rebound man came at the perfect time. I required a crutch that could help me fight the emotional loss of losing my son. I couldn't even get off the couch, let alone muster the strength to fight a battle. I met him on the party scene. He was ten years younger than I, and he was infatuated with me.

Now that I think about it, maybe it was a delusional concept from the beginning. The cougar–cub pairing was quite popular in my circle of friends. The two of us fit the description to a tee, and we worked it to our advantage. We both enjoyed the nightlife and party scene. Because we both used cocaine heavily, we felt that we understood each other and each other's needs. He wanted to be a man I could lean on and count on for financial support. He was thrilled about moving into my family estate, and he appeared to have the basics down. He worked, mowed the lawn, and always brought his drugs home.

I think I was hoping to walk down a road again that I had already walked down. But this time, I was going to do it with the proper partner. He was only twenty-two years old, and I wanted to correct my journey and do it right this time. Together, we waited out the time for my divorce to become finalized. We were engaged after a year and a half, married one year later (in 2005), and separated by 2010.

He had a statement to make to his God-fearing family, and I was used as a tool to express that desire. Had he spent more time paying attention to our marriage rather than jumping through hoops of approval from his father, maybe—and that's a big *maybe*—we would have had a fighting chance.

From the start, our situation was unhealthy. I don't know what we gained; it was just another marriage down the drain. It didn't even require Drano—how sad. I had lost my son to The Monster at the beginning of our relationship on December 24th, 2002. There was a lot of baggage that I brought into the relationship from the outset. It didn't help that we were both addicts for our own reasons. We were happy to live with blinders tightly secured to our false idea of a happy couple. We entered into a sacred commitment of marriage. Talk about ignoring all I had endured and learned up to this point in my life. I felt fearless because I was living in a world of drug abuse. It was easier to get high than admit the ugly truth, but in John 8:32, Jesus said, "Then you will know the truth, and the truth will set you free" (NIV). The truth shall set you free. *Freedom versus denial* seemed to be my issue of the decade, if not the past quarter of a century.

I found myself in court fighting for the custody of my son on Christmas Eve in 2002. I was completely heartbroken and turned to the new man in my life for support. He stood by me and continued to be a noble gentleman. He did accept and support this harshly damaged woman who had hit rock bottom. Sadly, his family thought I was the devil in disguise.

I will give credit where credit is due: he was only a twenty-two-year-old man, and he stood beside me. I was soon to be divorced and had a child custody battle on my hands. Despite the stress and blows that were being exchanged in the crossfire, Mr. Rebound was quite admirable. Maybe his determination to upset his father was more important. As for me, as long as my son wasn't by my side, I was empty and had no purpose or desire to do the right thing. Drugs became the foundation of our relationship.

The Monster had no problem putting me in the spotlight. *Humiliation* was my middle name. The Monster didn't lose any sleep regarding the welfare of our son; he saw custody as an opportunity to get back at me for destroying his world. The courts expected me to turn in regular drug-test information, and I had to pay for all of them.

Basically, I needed to remain clean and sober if I wanted to get my son back. I was broke and let the small empire I create fall apart. I worked incredibly hard to build a business that would support the three of us. When the separation between The Monster and I was finally in place, he refused to pay any child support. Plus, he expected me to split the business with him (the one *I* created and built). I figured that if he wanted to play, I would shut the doors. Nobody would share anything!

On December 24, I found myself in an eight-hour trial defending and fighting for the right of guardianship over my son. *Nightmare* was the word of the day! The judge awarded The Monster temporary custody, and I was allowed to visit with my child for three hours on Christmas Day. That visit was supervised. I couldn't believe it! I didn't help my case any when I told The Monster I was going to see him six feet under. As far as I was concerned, six feet under wasn't deep enough to bury him. I lost my cool, and he basked in the glory of my weakness.

It was Christmas morning, and I had been consuming drugs and alcohol all night long. I was not coping well, and I was entertaining a world full of misguided, angry energy. I was tired but determined to show up at the agreed-upon place for three hours with my son. After about two hours, I fell asleep. I woke up thirty minutes past our meeting time, and I began to panic. I couldn't believe I allowed myself to fall asleep.

Lady luck was not on my side as I left the place; however, she proved to be in my corner in the end. I was pulled over for speeding. If you have ever been pulled over for speeding on Christmas Day, you know the officers are never happy to be working that day. I was let off with a harsh warning, and then I was back on my way.

Upon arrival at The Monster's foster parents' home, I was looked at sideways. Despite the scrutiny from the audience, (parents, siblings, and friends), it felt good to feel my son in my arms! The smell of his energy was a blessing to me. He didn't seem too thrilled to visit with me, though, and he didn't have much to say. He knew I was late, and the look on his face said it!

I was not the person my son once thought I was. I had bought Christmas gifts for him with enthusiasm, but he was not impressed. The whole scenario was really awkward and strange. It was the first year I could remember not having a tree up in celebration of Christmas. When an eight-year-old child hurts you, it stays with you for life. I have not forgotten the feeling of desperation I felt then. My son had looked at me and stated that he wanted to live with his dad. My heart fell out of my stomach, and he squished it on the floor. I wondered, *what the hell just happened?*

I guess I deserve everything that was served to me on that day. There was no way I was upset with my child. Though he was never neglected or abandoned, I regret the damage I caused that innocent child due to my behavior. After all, his world had vanished in front of his eyes. I wanted to lash out, scream, and drive my car off the nearest cliff. I was an incredible fool to have put my selfishness before his emotional needs. It pains me today, and it is the only thing I would change if I had the chance to go back in my life to correct a wrong.

Later, I saw the woman who was once my mother-in-law. She looked at me and stated, "I cannot allow you to be alone with him." You can imagine the thoughts of disbelief that raced through my mind.

The next six months were a time that I could have done without. Spending eight supervised hours with my son every two weeks was like being sentenced to the hotbox and only being allowed fresh air and water when someone else saw fit. The visits and emotional frustration led these days of darkness for me. My family didn't understand what had happened, and I was not going to volunteer the information easily. I had not talked to my mother via telephone for a good eight months, and I avoided the issue. Hearing the disappointment in her voice would have driven me over the edge. After all, failure in any category was unacceptable to her. In the eyes of many, my reputation became another terrible issue.

Mr. Rebound was still at my side. We had been managing quite the emotional load, and I was a tad out of sorts. One day, we decided to crack open the bottle of mescal I brought home from my Mexican trip the year prior. It was a Sunday, and that's all I really remember. I woke up with the worm on my pillow and an empty bottle on the night table beside me.

The place was destroyed! I had never seen such destruction. There were holes up and down the hallway walls, pictures were ripped and broken on the floor. Mr.

Rebound was nowhere to be found, and the front end of my new sports car was crushed up like an aluminum can. I had cuts all over my legs, and my phone line had between severed. The next day, two officers rang the doorbell. They were wearing bright, canary yellow jackets, and I was oblivious about what had happened.

Still, I had cleaned up from the tornado that swept my house, so I invited them in. I couldn't understand why one of the officers kept eyeing my chest and other parts of my body. At the time, I thought they were being rude, and I chalked up the behavior to the stereotypical male response. Apparently, I had been in my car naked, crashed into the wooden telephone pole at the end of my block, and proceeded to drive back home as if nothing had happened. A neighbor witnessed me doing these crazy things.

When the police arrived at my house to investigate the offense, I was completely naked! Apparently, I told the cops where to go and how to get there. I gave them their budget too! They were unable to deal with me the day all my dignity was lost. I'm grateful they returned the following day because, after I apologized profusely, I showed them the empty liquor bottle of Mexican poison. They immediately understood my dilemma and changed their harsh tone. They could clearly see I was the victim of a very potent drug. I was given a couple of tickets, but I was lucky to come out of the situation alive. What if I had killed someone else or myself? It was another wrong turn. My dignity had vanished, and my neighbors were eyeing me sideways.

I wanted to run away as fast as I could and never look back. Mr. Rebound returned a few days later, and we were able to get past that horrible night.

Later, in 2003, it was time to pull up my socks and quit living a lifestyle of self-destruction. My son was living with The Monster, and I knew his true colors were starting to show. I became more willing to cooperate and wait for a window of opportunity. Supervised visits had ceased, and my son was spending the weekends with us. I had to rebuild our relationship, and it took several months to do that. He held my heart prisoner, and I blamed myself. His father could have negotiated a smoother transaction, but he made it as dramatic as possible.

Nevertheless, spending time with his father over those months allowed him to see what the man he idolized was really like. The window of opportunity opened when my son disclosed some information one weekend. He was in school, and it was the lunch hour. Some older boy had been harassing him for some time. When my son decided to stand up for himself that bully "tripped" and wound up chipping his tooth. When The Monster was notified, he became irate. He took our son by his neck and threw him up against the wall. My heart shattered into a million pieces. I wanted my son to see the truth and not be scarred and damaged by it.

It was time! I was clean and sober, Mr. Rebound man and I were stable, and my son (now nine) was ready to come home.

During the months I was working on evolving into a new and improved mother, I had the pleasure of getting to know Mr. Rebound's family. The outlaws were a bunch of hypocrites who belonged to a religious group, and I wanted to fit in. I was looking to be loved because I had been injured so badly. Before I met the members of his family, they had condemned me for being a divorced mother who was ten years older than their son. I was the Antichrist as far as they were concerned. I'm surprised they didn't refer to me as *Jezebel*.

Eventually, though, we started attending church and jumping through hoops for the family. We were expected to live and conduct ourselves in the manner they saw fit. Major issues, such as abstinence, were a real problem with them. There is one thing I am truly grateful for that occurred during the first nine years of my child's life: the gift I received when I became closer to the Lord. I studied my catechism for a year, and Mr. Rebound man and I married in their church in the summer of 2005. My son walked me down the aisle, and he couldn't have been prouder! The three of us were a family, and I was whole again. However, dark secrets about a double lifestyle eventually destroyed the rotten foundation that we had built. Our marriage was nothing more than a house of lies.

Chapter 6

Hard Times

A New Pathway to an Old Journey

As time escapes the day,
The distance will gather
A wall of bricks stacked up:
Regressions from what matters.

A back alleyway hidden by shadows;
Haunted is the passion of ignorance.
Potholes bruise a crippled trail;
One's own life without belief
Has no significance.

Humble are the steps that follow
The silhouette of a trail retraced.
Believing is knowing—
Not demanding to see.
Believe in yourself!

True faith for all of eternity.

My marriage to Mr. Rebound lasted four and a half years. Overall, the relationship was another eight years of wasted life for me. Leading a double life began to take its toll. We had a solid business that could have sustained a comfortable lifestyle. With my mother's wedding gift, a large sum of money, we started a mobile, auto paint, refinishing service.

From the beginning, we did really well together. Collecting customers was easy, and we built a solid foundation. Trying to remain focused and sober was a different story. Balancing a drug habit that extended into the next day became impossible to manage or conceal. Work was being neglected, which meant the financial end was dead. Every penny that was contributed to the home went to making sure dinner was on the table. That often entailed shopping at the dollar store. All other funds were negotiated to pharmaceutical prescriptions and the drug dealer.

After some time, Mr. Rebound fell into harder drugs that I could not stand to be around. Becoming a heroin addict is no joke. It controlled his life. Eventually, he began to lose his mind. Our wedding rings and other family jewelry wound up at the pawn shop. Bill collectors had been banging on the door, and our utilities were about to be cut off. He had been diagnosed with a combination of mental disorders, and there was no hiding or getting around his problems.

I chose to separate myself from that situation. Leaving him was not easy. I became broken once again—the relationship had taken another bite out of me. The domino effect wound up hurting everyone around us, including my mother. She donated money so we could live with normal amenities in our home. She wound up blaming me, and it took years before we could sit down as a mother and daughter should. I couldn't explain why the Visa card she had entrusted me with had well over twenty thousand dollars on it. How do you correct a situation that you never thought would occur?

Mr. Rebound was stealing from us right under my nose. I would put money into our joint bank account to cover monthly bills and business expenses. As I was going out the front door of the bank, he was coming in the back door and cleaning out the accounts. He would do this on the same day! I was too ignorant to see it at the time. Maybe the denial I so loved had a grip on me once again.

We ended up separating and getting back together a total of twelve times in one year. He had started to lose his mind in a very real way. He would lock himself in rooms and not come out for days on end. He would run away like a patient suffering from dementia. He would flick his cigarette ashes into my face. He would tower over me and scream in my face. When the verbal and physical abuse reared its ugly head, I decided I was done. I began to get the same feeling I had with The Monster. Although very different people, the two were both abusive, and I had enough memories from my first marriage to last me an eternity. I called in reinforcements from our Christian church and had him escorted out! I was stronger, and I felt no regret once I left.

Counseling sessions at four different clinics couldn't help us. I began to hate the man I was with and wanted nothing more to do with him or his family. The Christian church had become involved and tried to help, but they were unsuccessful. Leaving that marriage to endure what would come in the aftermath frightened me, but my son's happiness and my sanity were on the line. It brought me no comfort to face the music once again. *At least it didn't take me fifteen years to walk away,* I thought. *This time, it only took me eight.*

At that time, The Monster started knocking on the door, wanting to reconcile and be a family again. The last few years had taken a toll on him. He moved from house to house and couch to couch. The Monster was continuously in and out of relationships. He hoped we could reconcile, but I said, "No way!" He was also putting delusional concepts about the two of us into our son's mind. After a lengthy discussion with The Monster, he finally understood there would never be a future for us. He blew that.

Still, he kept promising me that he had changed, that he was a new man. He begged me to come back. I believe in my heart that he will never change. My son knew that, too, and he agreed that The Monster and I were better off alone. After all, he was sixteen, and he could see the reality of the outcome for himself. My baby boy was growing up.

Now that Mr. Rebound was gone, I had a chance to check out the damages. I began to sort through boxes and organize the house. After twenty years, it was time to salvage what was left of the family estate. I was there this time for my son, and he was there for me. I was not going to lose him again, and I did everything to make sure he knew we were going to get through the tough times ahead of us. I had no income, and the bills started to pour in. My hands were tied, and there wasn't a lot I could do. It was a time for reflection. I could honestly say my head was clear. My ears were no longer plugged with the pollution of abuse. I had finally arrived, and not a minute before my fortieth birthday.

I began to develop skills that I had suppressed in the past. I continued with my personal relationship with the Lord, and I'm so glad I did! Had I not derived my strength through the Lord, I would not have made it. I needed to be stronger than ever, and I leaned on the Lord.

Strength

Surrender to the power of self-control.
Threatening chaos will challenge our souls.
Retrieve the endearment, our vitality first.
Eternal food will quench our thirst.
Navigate the multitude of our own power.
Greatness and achievement every day, every hour.
Thrive and prosper, strengthen our mind.
Honesty and respect within ourselves to find.

My mother was unsympathetic to my situation. She couldn't understand my second marriage ending so soon or why large amounts of money were missing. She had the audacity to blame me. I remember talking to her via telephone and telling her I had left Mr. Rebound. With the cold response I was used to, she asked what I was going to do. I wasn't getting any younger, she noted, and she refused to help me in any way, shape, or form.

Why did I think I could lean on her? Because I always did. Mom was always there for me financially. It may have been easier for her to compensate for being an absentee mother by giving me money. After all, she left her life in Canada over twenty years ago. I misunderstood her. The strength she exuded and what she endured throughout her life was not insignificant, but she made it look easy. She always had a red coal burning in the fire, and heaven help anyone who challenged her. When Dad was alive, I remember her arguing with the sales clerks and cash register personnel. My dad was so graceful in terms of taking an awkward moment and making light of a situation. Even Mom had no choice but to resort to laughter. Dad basically gave his opinion to the surrounding ears. He said, "Ladies, get your boxing gloves on and duke it out the right way."

She had every reason to be disappointed in me. I was responsible for the man I brought into our lives. Someone needed to be held responsible. To this day, he has not taken responsibility for anything—not even the pills I found stuffed in the heater vents that he had stolen from me. I am thankful my dad was not around to see the mess that had been created. Daddy's little girl was a messed up, lost soul with insufficient strength left to repair damage that she was responsible for. Heartbreak and disbelief once again lined my soul.

Once she decided to grace us with her presence, she stayed with us for six weeks. Company traveled in from afar to visit her, and I put my damaged life on hold. Despite her attitude and self-proclamation that she was entitled to certain things, I sucked it up and put my best face forward. She made it perfectly clear that I had failed, that I was a failure. I thought, *how awesome is that? I love you too, Mom! You have not been a part of my life for over twenty years, and when you decide to drop by, you have the right to an opinion? I don't think so!* But I knew that standing up to her would ruffle her feathers because reminding her of my father would put a bitter taste in her mouth. Hey, I'll take that one as a compliment. Things were messed up; however, what got me through was my faith in the Lord and my great relationship with my son. It helped that he was older. It didn't soften the blow completely, but he could understand and accept the way things ended.

Chapter 7

SKELETONS IN THE CLOSET

When I look back through my childhood, I have many wonderful memories. I have enjoyed sharing them with my son. It wasn't the childhood from hell. I attended schools that left me with friends I still contact today. I have fond memories of being a part of a figure skating club. That made me who I am today to some degree. We had a great house with property that could stretch a child's imagination.

When thinking back, my mother spent quality time with us despite the fact that her career was always first. I do believe she loved her work more than us. Nevertheless, she remained faithful when it came to the care and welfare of her children. She handled her business and family brilliantly. I'm sure it wasn't easy for her.

Once, when I was only a toddler in diapers, my mother, brother, and I lived with close family members while she attended school after becoming a registered nurse. She wanted to further her career at that time, and she studied to become a public health nurse.

In the morning, she stood at the door and held a clear bag of red apples. I welled up with tears as I sat at the door and begged her not to leave. She handed me the bag of apples and said good-bye. This scenario, I am sure, is not a special occurrence—many children hate being left by their mothers. But I was treated so poorly by my family that it scared me for a long time.

I remember being kept in the root cellar often. We were neglected and confined to a small room with a cement floor, and a dim light bulb with a pull chain. I remember it was wet, cold, dark, and terrible. Out of sight, out of mind was the mentality.

I remember my older brother wrapping his arms around me and protecting his baby sister. He had a big brother quality that lasted throughout our teenage and young adult lives. I don't know how a child could be more protective than an adult. He got me through these times that seem almost impossible to think about. I was small and vulnerable, but the memories never stopped haunting me. Talk about skeletons in the closet!

There were times I thought I was put here on earth to suffer and be punished. I was then rescued and taken to my aunt's house. She had a good heart and loved us. However, it wasn't long before her husband started molesting me at the age of four. Why I was subjected to this abuse is absurd to think about today. It is not tolerated and not silenced. Had my dad known, I believe he would have killed the man. It was dealt with poorly and lasted for seven years.

I always felt threatened by the people who loved me the most. They were all cruel bastards and suffered little to no punishment for the heinous crimes they committed.

I grew up thinking I was not good enough the way I was. Even my mother hassled me about my grades and my weight. It's no wonder that, by the time I reached puberty, I felt so damaged.

My home life was brutal because Mom and Dad fought on a daily basis. They would argue, swear, and destroy our happy home. I then had a rather awkward teenage experience and hooked up with my first husband, The Monster, at sixteen. That added fifteen years to the abusive cycle. I became self-destructive and tainted my son.

And then I married another not-so-fabulous man. When that marriage failed, I left to start over again for the third time. The first half of my life sucked, to put it plainly. What the hell does anyone do to deserve such treatment? And how does society expect me to act now that I'm all screwed up?

Chapter 8
It's all about the Recovery

Now that I have shared some of the dirty details of my life, I don't expect sympathy. Rather, I hope I have spurred a willingness in you as an individual to make a difference for yourself and live the life intended for you. Too often, I have put myself second and somebody else first. I had no problem jumping through burning hoops that were held up high. I didn't realize that the consequences would be so devastating later in life.

Don't get me wrong. The energy provided to your children, significant other, and all other important people you tend to bend over backwards for is a good thing. We need to give in order to get back; we need to contribute to any relationship we choose to have. The energy I conveyed was misguided! I spent more strength trying to cover up my twisted truth than I did knowing right from wrong. If I had directed half of that energy toward protecting myself, maybe my story would have been different. Maybe I wouldn't be plagued with the nightmares that haunt my slumber.

It's not about beating ourselves up. Life has already claimed that space. We question our integrity regarding our own obedience. Every single command and wish our parents had for us weighs heavily because, face it, we always knew better. Or so we thought.

I now know I always thought I was the exception to the rule. I wanted to be the individual who was different, more special than all others who walked before me. How blinded I was. But dwelling on our mistakes will not bring back the past we screwed up. No one kicks harder than we kick ourselves. We are our own worst critics and enemies. We are responsible for the choices made throughout our life's journey no matter what.

Trust is a fragile word in my vocabulary. I can say through all my beatings, neglect, abuse, addiction, and trauma, I have not allowed the darkness that surrounded my life to have a final say today. So much has been lost and minimized in my journey thus far that I refuse to be a victim. And I will not victimize anyone who is vulnerable. To do otherwise is to let The Monster win.

Whatever life has left for this torn and battered soldier is not as dark as it once was. The strength now drawn from both dark days and light within has given me the strength to carry on with a smile on my face. Yes, I have addiction problems. Yes, I have nightmares that won't go away. Yes, I have regret. But I am happy because I didn't allow that ugly monster to win and take me away. I will continue to fight. I came from an era that paved the way for many cornerstones today. It wasn't for nothing!

It's all about the recovery. There is a time to mourn the past; there is a time to accept and reflect on what those lessons brought us. After that, there comes a time to move on. Allow the past to be a window of knowledge that can be used as gainful insight towards a healthier, happy life.

Sadness was accepted and acknowledged in my own journey when I was able to rise above all the madness that surrounded me. Yes, it does make one stronger; it does make one proud of where one came from and who one has become. Great strength and love are pulled from the depths of my own soul, and that is success in its own right—believing in myself! Everyone has the right to be happy and true to themselves. If we don't protect ourselves, who is going to? It's time to make a stand and love ourselves in our own entirety. Yes, we are worth the effort! Yes, we are worth the strength we possess and give to others.

Once we can love and honor ourselves, we can begin to love the rest of the world again. Getting off track is a normal part of life, but choosing to get back on track is up to us. Faith, hope, and happiness is possible.

Today, I am well and certain that all I endured was because the Lord knew I could handle it. There is much more to come from my journey, many more paths to choose, but I now know that I am mentally ready for the next chapter of my life. I will continue to hold my head up high and smile because no individual is going to take away what God instilled from the beginning.

There will be more mistakes, I am sure. I have found success with my son, who is now twenty years old. He has graduated from high school and spent a couple of years in college. We remain very close today as he travels along the pathways of his own journey. He doesn't have a relationship with his father today because he has his own personal reservations regarding The Monster.

I have regained trust and respect from my mother. Family has always been very important in my life's journey. It has kept me steady and true.

I have been in a new relationship since 2011. He is a man I have searched for my entire adult life. Although nobody's relationship is perfect, this one has been free of abuse. It may have taken me over forty years to arrive, but better late than never.

It feels great to have found Daddy's little girl again.

Daddy's Little Girl

It's a fresh new day
Time to make a choice
Should I remain bitter from the past
Or should I stand up to be a chosen voice

Should I dwell on the negative
Many would like to see me out of control
Haunted memories remind us
Why we have those scars on our souls

God gave us the gift of life
Many blessing He has bestowed
We are all unique and special
When He made us, He broke the mold

Life's lessons can be discouraging
Balancing the cruel with the kind
Learning to grow is the secret
In life there's no button to rewind

It's a new day the page is unwritten
Clean those tears off our pillows
Let us put our best foot forward
We shall leave the weeping to the willows

The End

About the Author

Lilian Grace is a new author with a story of her own to tell. She was born and raised in Canada, and she resides in British Columbia today.

About the Book

Daddy's Little Girl is an autobiography. It depicts the many turns that she made down the winding path and the obstacles that she overcame. It offers a positive message to readers. The poetry included reveals the inner depth of some of the experiences she endured. Come along on a journey that will describe the ups and downs—and some of the challenges that she was able to conquer.

CPSIA information can be obtained at www.ICGtesting.com
Printed in the USA
LVOW06s0756190215

427412LV00001B/13/P